The Pine-Woods Notebook

(after Francis Ponge)

Craig Dworkin

The Pine-Woods Notebook

(after Francis Ponge)

THE PINE-WOODS NOTEBOOK
BY CRAIG DWORKIN

Chicago: Kenning Editions, 2019

Kenningeditions.com

ISBN 978-0-9997198-4-8
Library of Congress Control Number: 2018953228

Distributed by Small Press Distribution
1341 Seventh Street, Berkeley, CA 94710

Spdbooks.org

Cover design and interior composition by Patrick Durgin.
Artwork: Tim Knowles, Tree Drawing - Scots Pine on Easel, Buttermere Shore #1, 2006. Ink on paper and C-type print 78 x 98 cm + 78 x 59 cm

This book was made possible in part by the supporters of Kenning Editions: Charles Bernstein, Julietta Cheung, Carol Ciavonne, Steve Dickison, Craig Dworkin, Kristin Dykstra, Laura Elrick, Jais Gossman, Kaplan Harris, Tom Healy, Lyn Hejinian, Kevin Killian, Edward McAdams, Krishan Mistry, Dee Morris, Chris Muravez, Sawako Nakayasu, Caroline Picard, Janelle Rebel, Kit Robinson, Jesse Seldess, Tyrone Williams, and Steven Zultanski.

Kenning Editions is a 501c3 non-profit, independent literary publisher investigating the relationships of aesthetic quality to political commitment. Consider donating or subscribing: Kenningeditions.com/shop/donation

For A.

When we hear the sound of the pine trees on a windy day, perhaps the wind is just blowing, and the pine tree is just standing in the wind. That is all that they are doing. But the people who listen to the wind in the tree will write a poem.

—Shunryu Suzuki

Only listen to the voice of pines and cedars
when no wind stirs.

—Ryonen Genso

The pitch of the pines on the ridgeline thickens, bewitching.

A needle drop announces with a bounce the delay in patience it anticipates.

Surface hiss risks rescinding its promise of prominence.

Wind's distance incites the pines to hush.

Silence correlates static.

From pine to sigh a sound propounds the ingrained impulse to perpetuate; the needling breeze yields, fecund and promiscuous.

An erratic passage of particles sibilates in an instant, dense spectrum; the more idiosyncratic their paths, the more uniform the impression of some cumulative constant; the drone then follows from a system out of tone.

With the wind at the margins, curvative tips serve to initiate rates of drag-induced lift; the silhouette's perimeter shimmers in the upwash.

Sap from the wavering sutures of bark, balsamic, darkens and brittles, black as shellac.

Propagating out in unheard annual vibrations, nested sets of xylographic lock-grooves loose slack dendral precessions, extending.

Handwriting offers, supine, consigning; an autograph co-signs, entrusting; a secant severs the substance; chords bisect chords; in the forms they construe, pens designate names — a sending away or removal of the referent yet retaining the same verbal regimens, of any nouns thought to be worthy of love.

Accidents inflect what a signature fixes.

Beneath the trees, a carmine fungus concentrates its muscarine.

The wind amands the seeds.

The sea demands its winter raft.

Ice, in its suspended retreat, mirrors the chare of the bay's tide's detray; a standing screen of Sitka intervenes.

Glacial melt aligns the drumlin hills with drifting till but scarcely alters the sound's salinity, which brines without relenting.

Salt saturates the sand culture; the grains refrain from seizing with the freeze.

The sound resigns, relinquishing liquidity to rink.

Wind frisks the crotchets of their last concealed desiccants.

Wedge-tailed shearwaters flight across wave fronts; remiges tailor the trimmed mersatorials.

Rews score the field with stitches; hedge and ditch grid the grassland past the ridgeline; an avenue of pendants rules the march.

Firs risk scalenity with suspending taliq scripts.

Excursus revokes heroic composure.

Pines rune.

Branches rine.

Every pining recks.

The thyrsus staves a cone with broken cane.

Limbs braid from their slumber at a gust.

The force wrakes out the unsound branches.

A winter storm havocks ice sheets and weed wracks from
their course.

Wakes burnish the sound with a sheen like the crease from
a bonefolder.

Spiculine leaves hone their sonic proportions; fundamentals
combine with their own harmonic overtones.

Stoic cortical rhytidomes corset the torsos.

The genus adapts from the alpine to the littoral.

A moisture exchange clearly alters the complexion of the
continent's constituents.

Pelagial salt settles, after it falls, dissolving, beneath
lacustrine calm.

Nutrients, sourced from soil, absorb.

The roots, without apology, appropriate the phosphates.

Certain literal phrases plagiarize an etymology.

A falcon's pinion angles, ruffles, and then resmooths.

Ochre chlorosis transmits the tips' deficiency; they twist
from want of copper in the silicate alkaline silt.

Contaminants accrue. Etiology accuses.

Water sounds the soil.

A trunk frets the shallows, leisurely autistic, keeling with
the heaves. Surf worries the fibrous pith, easing the
sleeving from the trunk.

Late season's waning sun cedes to altostratus — and
etiolates.

The old-growth browns lack luster from the brack; fresh
green foliage gleams like jade; needles shine in perennial
foison.

Bark husks harden and slough; they curl in quarter pipes:
the felled fine pelt of a tall, unfortunate and fatal pine.

Discarding, dative, pencil cedar and native deal peel
impermanent worm-etched stencils.

Methyl jasmonate accumulates up phenylpropanoid paths;
resins run rising along the corridors; phenolic plant
flavenoids travel rapidly back, building metabolic shields;
they synthesize in sympathetic paranoia. Chalcone
enzymes modulate the terpenoids.

From their simple harmonic motions, needles sough in the soft breeding breeze.

With a dissipate flare, the toroid sings in rounds. The ring of the sound — its particular pitch, intensity and timbre — radiates down in a widening vortex.

The pyrexial curve of earth steadily rises, without any remittance, then plummets, diurnal, in turns of duly even undulations.

From the bank, down the cashel, the forest floor patterns its parquetry without any smooth planks, without a single washed board, but with the thickest of carpets. The cushioning spread of the dead softens the pack of the soil.

The mesh of needles belies the firmness of the live wood's muscular flesh.

The valve of the pyxis' amphora attaches the axis like a one-handled amber.

Wild ache laces the base of the lease, mascling the field, purling the vert, juvating the shade's proximity — everything jagged, cut, and vittered.

A wrap of sapwood protects the core.

Capillary pressure acts against gravity.

The sun sounds the shade, appraising the tightness of the laced needles' braiding.

The dark of the trunks predates the dusk.

The pitch of the outline as it climbs to the cyma defines the cast of the profile and its iconic geometry: a pyramid rotated to a cone more perfect than the form of any pines' eponymous seedpods.

Little circles of shadow polka the brule beneath evergreen parasols.

Naked, seeds scatter, candid, in the breeze.

The listener harkens as the echo falls off.

The waves recede as the troughs increase.

Currents rancor the strand's sand's crust.

Pointed needles punge.

The porous screen breathes.

Blister-rust fungus ochers the cankers from obligate currants.

Boughs bow, catenary, and low; they bob and nod in conference.

Skyview factors the fraction of a field's saturant blue.

Connate forms connote a rote geometry of geminate digression.

In its fluid motion through a pressure Hessian the wind courts quaternions as negative scalars; the decrement of density at any point calculates a marked divergence.

A chorus distributes what the single needle focuses.

The continuous whisper of psithurisma varies by the schist.

The pine's structure cancels what it best produces, quieting the very music that it makes.

Again and again, one finds the consensus: nothing is better suited to wind than the pine.

But in conifers connection to the wind is always more than musical. The pine reminds with its sigh that it needs the wind to reproduce, to pursue its genetic impetus; it requires dissemination but cannot rely on birds or insects for its pollination. Wind deterritorializes the sexual organs of these trees.

Against the trunk's tower and the acclivitous thrust of the boughs the branchlets depend, perpendicular, imitating the fall of the rain they maintain.

The greaves receive their shade.

On one anomalous sapling, five branch-sets cincture the timber in rungs.

Sap taps from the cambium, viscid and succulent. As the resin warms an amber tinctures.

Pitch follows hews.

Pine trees pulsate between the graves.

The sigh of the pines ensues from the wind.

The wind of vines branks the trunk's bark's enlargement.

Snows grieve the evergreens at certain elevations. A verduant limb hitches at the vector's divergence. The power of the fit factors the pack of the powder.

The walkers stop, unsure, for a moment, if they're within hearing of a stream or if the wind's picked up in the trees — then, a certain movement in the needles' vertical curtain confirms.

After the sea, the serene beauty of the pine is by far the most celebrated singing.

Pine needles trouble the laminar motion — and muddle.

A trobellion develops a rotative course; the tortative storm envelops the valley.

A model of passion devalues abstraction.

Compounding sounds disallow the impulse, before really listening, to describe it as a *roar*, or a *rumble*, or the *billowing of sheets*.

On reflection, the sigh is heard as the sound of pure statistics, the audible slope of stochastics, the reason the sough of the water and the wind in the trees seem often indistinguishable.

An angle of inclination establishes axes; each clinical lack stakes a kind of attraction; every set with time tends.

Calculus mocks the mathematics of the pine, describing the endless desire to approach, ever closer, to the unattainable.

In the end, there is the vast number and there is the clinamen — that's all: the noise of the cascade, in the spray's chance dance of myriad droplets, and that inclination, from high to low, which produces movement, and which makes meaning — because it is the meaning of movement — in the crush of signs.

Accounting for variables, the slope of the probable models its parable.

The impression of sighs rounds the sound.

For the cypress, the bough's sweep counters the weep of the branches.

A needling partitions the cant's tilt: akimbo, acute.

Boles pose as posts — or climb as pillars, or columns — steepling the seeds.

Two owls pire above the planceer of a branch.

Spruce spires lanch the much lighter blue.

Some few suffice to diffuse the sunlight's stifle.

In fields, aromas arise with the temperature, and then dissipate; under pines they suspend in the fresh, maintaining.

Conifers sparse odors as they cool, so that the temperature, inseparable from their scent, suffuses.

With a gentle breath of aryl hydrocarbons, pines aspirate against every aridity, biding the season with a harbor against heat.

Something gently vibrating — sweetly balanced and musical — sweeps the stand.

Volatile aromatics atomize; accretion reactions escalate; hydrogen abstracts; low volatility vapors acuate the condensates.

Though the pitch of perfume has less to do with smell — a deeply sensual matter — than pure wish fulfillment, it is a whole communion of perfumes, of thoughts and of breathing which attach us to these trees as to no others.

Camphoraceous bornyl acetate esters accrete.

Aerosols bloom above boreal forests.

The hazel snakes its roots.

A fine net laces its way toward a cloud.

The vapor leads to haze.

Everything continues to cool beneath the canopy.

For a spell, as after waking, the sting of paræsthesia tingles a ringing static of haptic sensation.

At rest, in the shade, the compressing chest concentrates the rasp of respiring.

The wind, heaving, avails its leafing.

Rushes mime, from a distance, along the marsh's perimeter.

Sheer pressure is audible beneath the turmoil of the slope-layered race of chaos in the flow regime; one is hearing, in fact, the *absence* of whatever might have blocked the wind, or been moved by it. Ears' cavities amplify ambient resonance; they echo the hush of a pulsant tinnitus.

Glabrous, with prominent pulvini, needles glaucous above a few stomata, glucosides seeped in the bark, the Sitka linger in the low clouds.

Even deciduous ribs reach like needles, debossed in the webbing of outspread leaves.

Cones pake the hard-pack cake of the soil, and recoil.

Soft mocks of sedge tufts smudge the plain.

Old-growth weaves a shading screen in wraps of looming, waving drapery.

Pies vaunt, pontificating, and vie for vantaged heights; they happer back from crown to bough and declare in their pompous, opinionated ways. Brisk, smart and lively, preening, exceedingly trim — their formal tails starch, neat and dapper.

A key's tangent determines the pitch of the note and narrows attack; its attitude, like a neutral glance, falls gallant and balanced.

But then a quick wince at a pang of remorse, some aculeus combined with a fleeting anxiety — the littlest ache from panic mixed with fear — leads to guilt at the stipple of a bit lip's lingering wale's refusal to dissipate.

Rosin tempers the brilliance of the tone and damps the attack, from *hart* to *weichen* to an open decay; the syncopation's gradation anticipates the stroke of its echo's impended delay.

Velic closure baffles the airflow to cavities.

Lac-resin waxes the strands.

The angle relents.

Lenitions loosen, with a soft mutation, each mention's muffled articulation.

The ankle's tattoo, with its archaic alphabet laid over veins, silently traces the mute arabesques of the sandal's loosed laces.

The turn of the neck and the curve of the legs disposes the body, weightless, in sustained levitation; the amber complexion of the pale trunk rises; the spine elongates with impossible vertebrae.

The back tenses, arcs forward, and the convex relaxes.

Flourished incisions purfle the pine from the luthier's furl.

The calculus curl of the f-hole scrolls its approach: serpentous, pursuant.

The hand-inked print inscribes the logic of the negative itself on the image's surface: trunk turned to front, at once, as the trunk, *a tergo*, retracts its effacement.

The reversal repeats until any differentiation is lost between the shadow and the wind's pitch.

The instant fit of a vacillating needle mimes the mark left on skin when it's bitten.

A pine valley disposes its vaporal gradients bathed beneath layers of slow exhalations.

Auriferous quartz, in the curve of an anticline, tapers in every direction.

The switch-back curves from the vertebra, linking the slopes and the saddles sinking from the crinkle.

The tack of the pitch reduces the friction of what it attracts.

Needles stitch the careless collision.

Bark wounds ooze.

The viscid sap's grasp expands, then contracts.

The bruise models it blue on the halo, now extinct, from the lingering sting of inked needles.

A branch's proclivity fancies a whim; composition conforms; needles, thin as minims, justify themselves with the tight composure of typed lines of characters spaced in arrays in a uniform size.

The pitch of the type determines the density.

Once pieceous essence was used to make printer's ink; but almost every modern writer began, via sized sheets of wood pulp, with a certain sort of forest language.

Every ending expunges a tending.

The fertile is heard as a wishing.

The nets of the needles' shadows are cast.

The fir trees' pinnacles focus infinity.

Beneath an even diffusion lies a darker pungence.

To listen to the pitch is to hear the list in the piston of the spinney's lisped, established combination of slides and stops: appetite, craving; desire, longing; revolution, revolution.

Trunks serve as staples to the branches' reeds.

The scored bark records the pitch; its precise placement and expression are predetermined by the lines.

A makeshift hurtle furthers the shadows; stems wend the wind; dampened pine withes writhe as they dry.

A sigh is the perfect expression of a pine. It professes, variously: imprecation, emphasis, joy, sadness, and anger; surprise and warning; wonder and admiration; compassion, pain, impatience, doubt, again surprise and admiration, sadness, and irony — ultimately, always, some sort of physical and emotional suffering.

More numerous species of conifers form a chorus; their frequency increases as they climb, as high as the tree-line's limit.

Pine boughs pitch in the blistering wind, even when their trunks maintain a distanced indifference.

The breeze bestows a certain eloquence to pines, but they speak only in terms of slow spreading rumors and quick bit lips, successions of crescendo and diminution, of their benefactor's ceaseless cycles of arrival and departure, announcing insistently the possibility of its own enunciation.

Yet the wind in the trees is a sheer velleity, expressing their mere wish, desire, or inclination without any accompanying action or effort on their part. The wind is just blowing, and the pine tree is just standing in the wind.

The sigh defines: to yearn; to wish, to languish with desire, to long for with an ever even more eager hunger. The index is negative, set, and strict.

Sitka fret the strand.

Engelmann Spruce disperse themselves eastward, as far as the Rockies.

The easy confusion of conifers, despite the manifold deviates, persists against stock particulars: the juniper, the fir and the cypress together, the deforested cedar, the spruces and yews. An afterimage of division remains as the species recede.

I have tried all kinds of pines with much the same results, every different kind giving different timbre, still each kind being perfect regards tone, to find that pitchpine is more brilliant and powerful than all others.

Catenaries mirror, inversely, the cambers.

The wind, now, receding, is found outside the pines and cedars.

The list of the pitches evinces a wish for the roll of persuasive proposals.

The forest catches the faintest snatch of needles, obliquely, falling in a sound. They spiral as they swoon and then, before resting, hapax, rebound.

Shed needles nestle in a spread of sheltered beds, haphazardly carpeting each conical grade with a seasonal chronicle.

At some point, this piqued interest in pines will seem also a sting, a mote, a tear, some little hole — and also a throw of the dice.

The oracle's leaves speak in complete incoherence — unmeasured, irregular, inarticulate sibilants; only after the fact do the priests assign meters; the Sybil resists any hint of explicitness, however delicious, but the priestess insists.

Chance patterns, xylomantic, enchant: the low rustle against sigh; the frantic chatter of the scatter; a subsequent silence; the rise and fall with which the forest seems, for a spell, together to descant.

Pines damp what the grasses amplify.

The copse sings with a shimmering musicality, agreeable and sweet.

The chorus, chanting, entrances; the forest reprises; the piner refrains; the aura, plangent, fades and abates.

A certain very fine air or wind finds its way — by errant dint makes out a path — and explores among the ponderosa.

A weight of conscience reckons among the conifers; the walker reflects, wonders, and thinks the matter over before reaching a conclusion — he makes a decision and then holds openly forth, continuing the canyon's copse's course.

Inaudibly, pitch-tipped needles tattoo their detail to the switch; they pattern the bed of the bend.

Just beyond the sylvan stream, the sap secretes like melatonin, disrupting the rhythms of the day.

The pitch of the pines darkens the daytime.

Waves lace the brace of the sea.

Under breeze, the lancing branches blanch.

The music of the spruce mounts from spumid to acute.

A sieve of discriminating needles lue disseminating currents. Their cernicle scries as a searce; the cribble siles the range of the winds as a riddle filters certain sounds clean out.

Limbs shift in wind to sift, discretely, its noises into tones; their bolting garbles and gathers the notes into noise once again; a soft musical accompaniment, muted, acuminates.

Cast by chance on the carpet, shards of shadow spill from

the coppice and, appalling, dispel — they scant as they scatter, then pool again, impelled by scintillæ to spall.

The saunter of the pattern trances.

The tamis anthers sparge.

The perse of the spruce fades from bice to argentate to azurine to blue.

Seed pods trip in rings their timber weights.

Winds strip the weeds in spates after simmers.

The breeze then decreases the stress of its shearing with an audible fall: an initial ictus, beginning with the arsis, descending to the thesis.

The wistful, listening, anticipate.

An isthmus pierces the sweep of the sea.

A scrim of conifers fringes the inlet.

Firs, frim, meld and fret in the liquescent air; the humidity films as the spinet perspires.

One day in the middle of the third month of the terror, the season outpaces the cool of the pines.

Plates flake in florescence, with nested coronas of cone-frozen petals.

The sea slowly ventures new frets toward the forest.

The pitch of the pines transfixes the plane of the brim.

The shire strait sharpens the dap of the shadows, the dance of the ackers, the curls on the surface that scatter like drakes.

The pitch of the pines on the shoreline rises, shadowing a sound.

A tone makes allowance for long-standing alliance.

Wind purges and prunes, decards and reshuffles, folds and redresses the weeds with its undulant surges. They protest by histing the listener's attention.

Vengeful clergions jewel the crown of the conifer, circling the verge in a vocal corvine versicle.

Aranyaka raises ritual; *ashoka* pillars prone.

A harrier hawk, pausing, pursues by acoustics; it harkens, auditions the prairie, and hones.

Winds hew the meadow's extremities.

Turning, with sighs, far spiral firs he sees.

Tasseled grasses ascertain wind's quick-shifting compass; its hassling tousles the mane of the hawse.

The foxtail swivets.

The mouse finds its hulster.

Wood melic swells into full-crested billows.

Reeds sing with mellifluous sweetness.

Deliberate bees repace the stalks' obstacles; in the space between waves, panicles and racemes of sparsely flowered spikelets clasp at their passing.

Pitches tip, toping and seem to arrest the parsemé sparkles: the flow-angle yearns for a drainage, longs after, and caves into craving.

Inebriated pines run away forever. The whole forest sings. The tree musicians occasionally fall silent but the voice of the wood is always equally loud.

Needles aspen the evening's convection; the pent branches throb; slack grasses fluster at the bluster of the air's fluctuation.

A seep marks the degree with which *Sap*, the *Cortical Body* being dilated as far as its *Tone*, without a solution of Continuity, will bear; and the supply of the *Sap* still renew'd: the purest part, as most apt and ready, recedes, with all its due *Tinctures*.

A liquid elixir of pine pitch mixed with pitch-pine switches quickens.

Nicks, in this instance, indicate the pitch, the degree from the level, the rise of the drink, the direct bend of the sink in the leading of clay or soft soil; *corfes*, in this context, are falsely inferred as the gaps between hills.

A tuning-fork tines the blur of the spectrum.

An A, an F, an E, then . . . a stillness — the three proceed to trace the ineffable feeling of a breath of wind waning.

The pitch sets the tone of the pine, the particular inflexion of its voice expressing some feeling or emotion.

The sigh, depending, signs sorrow, distress or grief; the trees make entreaty, appeal, or remonstrance; initially, they signal some realization, discovery, or inspiration; and then: pleasure, surprise, wonder, or admiration — and in the end, a resignation.

Conifers, persistent, vacillate without the vast impatience of deciduous plants. After a certain hesitation, needles in tempest, intemperate, palpitate.

The light rakes, then levels.

Wagers stake against the hazard of the cast.

Spaced even as pales the boles range like fence poles.

Horizontal, the set holds — then clines.

The scent of the ranks, resinous, settles.

Bark, in a few curls, coffers the trunk.

Needles net in the damp; pitch echoes and resonates.

The first shadow on the cliff's rock sets the red-hawk's curfew.

The dark confirms the conifers' density.

Officious *pica*, pert, perk and swanker.

I am always surprised by the pitch of the pines, even in daylight; their silhouettes are absolute against the set.

The base of the bank breaks, unlacing the sky's horizon;
needles sprinkle the smoulder's glow.

The firs gather amber between their needletips and start to
articulate the lateness of the day.

Branchlets temperate the light, and some wind.

Resins retard the consummating rate.

The trees' feigned indifference to the season makes us forget
that their needles are leaves, and imagine they never
fall, when in fact they are just exceedingly patient and
perfectly paced, waiting, at an annual rate, slow beyond
notice, and relieved only when their own replacements
are ready.

The relation, deceiving, redefines: to lie, or practise
deception; to evade a duty, to malinger.

In effect, the trunks' rectitude suggests their sheer
indifference to the sun: no inclination to correct for the
declination of the light's ellipsis' drift — no inkling of a
compensation for the radiation's wane.

A cyme styles, analemmatic, the dial of the bottom's
branches' skirt.

The densest busks of twigwork form a hurdle.

Discarded needles coat eroded soil.

Beached driftwood hurts the curve of the bay's rondelled
azure.

Everything, abraded, wears away.

Winds lay the staggered mesas spoil.

The juniper purges its branches of fruit.

The storm rusks the thorns.

The wind, in the end gains a purchase, and — surging — uproots.

The pine, which is born in the mountains, where it is quickly overcome by winds, is often carried off into gardens, where it is easily hewn by the self-same violence.

The trees weep from their scales, and at the bracts of their catkins.

Brume cumbers cumulate brakes.

The coombe from the seacoast lunates the verge.

Solutes pass through the symplast of the vascular xylem.

Larchen slopes parch from continuing drought.

Stone arrests deficient adventitia; the persistent underground members resist.

A harrier hides in its asylum blind.

The stolen and escaped evade.

The détourned reroutes the taken and the left.

Fugitives maroon in new communities.

The lacking tufts the flanching canopy.

Obligates reduplicate the duties of the holden.

But the forest lies always *outside* of the law that creates it: off limits; uncultivated; beyond its own repurposed pales; exceeding the purview of the legislated civil.

The pitch, as a liquid, seeks its own level. The flow lasts as long as the vessels communicate.

Several denotations are seduced to commute.

A woodpecker wrecks its own rhythm, then resumes, remarking the bark with a patterned tattoo; from a distance, its partner harks to the arc of the patter, then answers. The skin of the tree receives the meter of the beak.

The atmosphere thins and pertains to the curtaining skirting the ancient coast's stand: at a certain altitude, a single species, entirely pine, pervades. The rigid pitch of the alpine cliffs inhibits the soil from seeding.

A perfumed breath lingers, out of reach of the heat.

Bursts of needles splay with an abstracted radius. The larch's fascicles finger in asterisk fans.

Certain hues blur, blend, and tinge when the light plays and bends on the plights of a span in particular ways.

The needles' course models the curve of the spine.

The skin, porous, absorbs the last fragrance.

To grasp what one doesn't dare touch courts desire.

The supine rises, erect, to embrace — and resists.

The proximate, delaying, risks promising the anticipant kiss
it purloins.

The lasting remains.

The endless accusative echoes, in feigned perpetuity, a
deferring decay denoting its purpose.

Even the bit lip confesses; its silence licenses simple
dismissals; the salience pouts and addresses.

Resigning desire cultivates pining.

The silen, in fancy — dazed, drowsing — now dozes.

The forest discloses the strone's summer's slumber.

Amber, archival, sustains some moment of lost frozen
violence, as a photograph, Faustian, wagers nostalgia.

To recognize the sign's desire for expression is to prize the
regression from pitch to rhythm to resonance.

A tree seeks its own unsustainable height, by gradation.

The leaves wait the season; the sap refines.

The sigh, as pure affect, respires the sign.

The size of the pines determines the spacing arranged by
the strand's stand's rank.

A resolve equates with a perfect proportion, and cancels its
ratios.

The plagal cadence still heralds suspension's refusal in a final
surrendered concess.

Aspiration, unappeasing, acquiescent, recedes.

The fleeting breeze betrays the trees.

The insatiable frustrates its statement's conclusion.

One finds in the send sound's requisite echo, proleptic.

And then, for a moment, again: the pines' pitches —
aligning — define.

Cascades/ Wasatch
14 November, 2014

If I say "I saw a pine tree on the road," and you say you understand the word *pine* tree, do you mean you know all the rules of the word. Are they all in your head when you say this?

—Ludwig Wittgenstein

NOTES

"When we hear the sound of the pine trees … ." Shunryu Suzuki: *Zen Mind, Beginner's Mind* (Boston: Shambala, 2011): 65.

"Just listen to what the pines and cedars say on a windless night." *The Hidden Lamp: Stories from 25 Centuries of Awakened Women*, ed. Florence Caplow, Susan Moon, and Zoketsu Norman Fischer (Somerville: Wisdom Press, 2013): 118.

"A moisture exchange … ." *Cf.* "Cambium humiditas manifeste alterata membri continentis complexione." Arnauld de Villeneuve (as cited Émile Littré: *Dictionnaire de la langue française* (Paris: Hachette, 1877): *Speculum introductionum medicinalium*, in *Opera omnia*, ed. Nicolas Taurellus (Basel, 1585): 13.

"A trunk frets the shallows … " The emblem of Giovan Francesco Macasciuola, which featured the device of a pine beset by the four winds and the motto *Quid in pelago?* takes the affinity of wind and pine to metonymically equates conifers with ships tossed by the stormy sea, since the latter's masts are made of pine and their hulls sealed with pitch. *Cf.* Susan Gaylard:

Hollow Men: Objects and Public Image in Renaissance Italy (Bronx: Fordham University Press, 2013): 257-258. An associated descriptive verse by Lodovico Dolce hints at the disseminating role of the wind for conifers; it opens: "Percuote il Pin di gravi frutti pieno /Forza di venti [The full fruit of the winds' severe force strikes the pine]" [Giovanni Battista Pittoni: *Impresse di diversi precipi, duchy, signori e d'altri personaggi et huomini letterati e illustri,* Vol. II (Venice: 1566): np.]. *Cf.* Torquato Tasso: *Opere di Torquato Tasso: con le controversie spora La Gerusalemme Liberate: e con le Annotazioni intere di varii Autori, notabilmente in questa impresione accresciute*, Vol. VII (Venice: Steffano Monti 1737): 79. *Cf.* "The loftie pyne tree was not hewen from mountaines, where it stood/ In seeking straunge and foren landes to rove upon the flood" [Arthur Golding: *The XV Booke of P. Ovidius Naso, entytuled Metamorphosis, translated oute of Latin into English meeter*, (London: Willyam Sers, 1567): Book I, l. 109].

"Pine trees pulsate between the graves." *Cf.* "les pins palpite entre les tombes" [Paul Valéry: "Le Cimetière marin," *Œuvres,* tome I (Paris: Gallimard, 1962): 147].

"The forest floor patterns its parquetry ... ." *Cf.* "(Sans planche lisse au sol)/ Sans planches lavées au sol mais des tapis épais" [Francis Ponge: *Le carnet du bois de pins* (Lausanne: Mermod, 1947): 18].

"unfortunate and fatal pine." Thomas Kyd: *The Spanish Tragedy*, ed. J. R. Mulryne (London: Black, 1990): IV: 2, l. 7.

"Wild ache ... ." *Cf.* " The wilde Ache or Parseley hath large leaves, al jagged, cut, and vittered, much like the leaves of the wilde Carrot." H. Lyte: *A niewe herball, or historie of plantes, first set foorth in the Doutche tongue*, trans. R. Dodoens (London: E. Grifin, 1619): 609.

"Nothing is better suited to wind than the pine." Liu Chi: "Wind-in-the-Pines Pavilion," *Inscribed Landscapes: Travel Writing from Imperial China*, trans. Richard Strassberg (Berkeley: University of California Press, 1994): 281. Chi goes on to explain: "when wind passes through it, it is neither obstructed nor agitated. Wind flows through smoothly with a natural sound." The trope is common across cultures. Consider, for just one example: "what purely natural sound appeals more to the imagination than the wind in pine-trees?" [Caroline Fothergill: *Diana Wentworth: A Novel* (New York: Harper Brothers, 1889): 74]. This conflation is perhaps what Augusta Larned refers to as a "summer philosophy": "a philosophy of trees and flowers, of moving cloud shadows, bird-songs, waving grass, and rippling waters, the sound of breakers on the shore, the murmuring wind in pine-trees" [Augusta Larned: "A Summer Gospel," *The Christian Register* 8 (26 July, 1900): 819].

"After the sea, the serene beauty of the pine is by far the most celebrated singing." *Cf.* "Après la mer, le chant trois célèbre le pin à la beauté sereine," Rene Cuzacq: *L'époque contemporaine, 1919-1949* (Éditions Jean-Lacoste, 1950): 49. *Cf.* "The sea was near at hand, but not intrusive; it murmured, and he thought it was the pines; the pines murmured in precisely the same tones, and he thought they were the sea" (Thomas Hardy: *Tess of D'Ubervilles: A Pure Woman Faithfully Presented* [New York: Harper & Brothers, 1893]: 431).

"Wind deterritorializes the sexual organs of these trees." *Cf.* Gilles Deleuze and Félix Guattari: *Capitalisme et schizophrénie: milles plateau* (Paris: Éditions de Minuit, 1980): 360; 17; *et passim*.

"In the end, there is the vast number and there is the clinamen ... ." *Cf.* Michel Serres: "The Genesis of Sense," *The Birth of Physics*, trans. Jack Hawkes, ed. David Webb (Manchester: Clinamen Press, 2000): 144-147.

"Conifers sparse odors as they cool, so that the temperature ..." *Cf.* Ehn, Mikael, et al.: "A Large Source of Low-Volatility Secondary Organic Aerosol," *Nature* 506 (27 February, 2014): 476-479.

"Something gently vibrating — sweetly balanced and musical — sweeps the stand." *Cf.* "On est très bien là-dessous, tandis qu'aux faîtes il se passe quelque chose de très doucement balancé et musical, de très doucement vibrant." Ponge, *Carnet*, 17.

"The pitch of perfume has less to do with smell ..." *Punch* 290: 2 (1986): 32; "it is a whole communion of perfumes ..." *Cf.* "c'est tout une communauté de parfums, de pensées et de souffle qui nous rattache à ces êtres comme à nuls autre" [André Breton: "Les Visages de la femme," *Man Ray: Photographies 1920-1934* (Paris: Cahiers d'art, 1934)]. *Cf.* Francis Ponge's sense of the pine's "parfum discret" [Ponge, *Carnet*, 13; 24].

"But then a quick wince ... ." *Cf.* Littré at *pinçon*.

"... mute arabesques ... ." *et seq.*. *Cf.* Robert Rosenblum: *Ingres* (New York: Abrams, 1990): 66.

"the amber complexion ... ." *Cf.* "Rembrandt lui-même envierait la couleur ambrée de ce torse pale." Frères Goncourts: "Le 'Bain Turc' D'Ingres," *Gazette des beaux-*

arts XXXVI (Paris, July 1906): 182; "… . impossible vertebrae." *Cf.* the "vertèbres supplémentaires" often attributed to the similarly distended back of Ingres' *Grande Odalisque* (though the exact number varies according to the critic, from two to some to several). Auguste Hilarion (comte de Kératry) counted three: "son *Odalisque* a trois vertèbres de trop," he was said to have told Eugène Emmanuel Amaury Pineu Duval [*L'atelier d'Ingres* (Paris: Champetier, 1878): 370]. More recent studies have adduced up to five [Jean-Yves Maigne, Gilles Chatellier and Hélène Norlöff: "Extra vertebrae in Ingres' La Grande Odalisque," *Journal of the Royal Society of Medicine* 97: 7 (July, 2004): 342-344].

"… between the shadow and the wind's pitch." *Cf.* Joseph Massey: *Areas of Fog* (Exeter: Shearsman Books, 2009): 3.

"… the mark left on skin when it's bitten." *Cf.* Littré at *pinçon*.

"… every modern writer began … ." *Confer* the quite different sense intended by "il n'est guère d'écrivain qui ne soit menacé par la langue de bois." Maurice Mourier: "Pour une langue de cryptoméria," *Riveneuve Continents: Revue des Littératures de Langue Française* 1: 3 (2005): 11.

"… the fir and the cypress together … ." *Cf.* Isaiah 60: 13.

"I have tried all kinds of pines with much the same results … ." Byford: "On Violins," *English Mechanic and World of Science* Vol. XLVII No. 1,198 (9 March, 1888): 33.

"The copse sings … ." *Cf.* "une musicalité vibrante mais douce et agreeable." Ponge, *Carnet*, 13.

“A certain very fine air or wind … .” *Cf.* René Descartes, *Oeuvres de Descartes*, ed. Charles Adam and Paul Tannery Vol. XI (Paris: Vrin, 1974): 331.

“A soft musical accompaniment … .” *Cf.* “Bruits, musique discrète […] doux accompagnement musical en sourdine.” Ponge, *Carnet*, 24.

“… will seem also a sting … .” *Cf.* “c’est aussi: piqure, petit trou, petite tache, petite coupure — et aussi coup de dés.” Roland Barthes: *La Chambre claire* (Paris: Gallimard, 1980): 49.

“ Turning, with sighs, far spiral firs he sees.” Richard Savage: “The Wanderer,” *The Poetical Works of Richard Savage with the Life of the Author* (New York: William Davis, 1805): 40.

“Inebriated pines run away forever … .” *Cf.* “Les pins ivres fuguent toujours. Toute la forêt chante. Les arbres musiciens s’écroulent de temps en temps mais la voix de la forêt est toujours aussi puissante. La vie commence” [Jacques Stéphen Alexis: *Les arbres musiciens* (Paris: Gallimard, 1957): 392]. Alexis’ novel concludes: “Life begins.”

“A seep marks the degree … . “ Nehemiah Grew: *The Anatomy of Vegetables Begun, Book II* (London: Hickman, 1672): 52.

“Branchlets temperate the light, and some wind.” *Cf.* “températion de la lumière,/ du vent.” Ponge, *Carnet*, 24.

“The pine, which is born in the mountains … .” *Cf.* “Il Pino, che nasce ne’ monti, ne’ quali agevolmente è superato da’ venti, suol esser trasportato ne’ giardini’, dove di ieggieri è crollato dall'istessa violenza." Torquato Tasso: *Delle Opere di Torquato Tasso, con le controversie sopra La Gerusalemme Liberata, et con le Annotazioni intere di vari Autori, notabilmente in questa impression accresciute, Vol. VII* (Venezia: Steffano Monti, 1737): 79. *Cf.* the Scots term "muckle forester" for a wind so strong it can uproot trees.

"The taken and left ... ." *Cf.* "The ones that get took// the ones that got left." Fred Moten: *Hughson's Tavern* (Providence: Leon Works, 2008): 19.

"Fugitives maroon ... ." *Cf.* the relation between needle and slave: "Gif ðu fioh to borge selle þinum geferan, þe mid þe eardian wille, ne niede ðu hine swa swa niedling" (*Laws of Ælfred*, Introduction, xxxv : 38 [Corpus Cambridge 173]).

"The piner refrains." *Cf.* "*piner*: a penetrating cold south-easterly wind." Bill Griffiths: *Fishing and Folk: Life and Dialect on the North Sea Coast* (Newcastle upon Tyne: Northumbria University Press, 2008): 36.

"If I say... ." Ludwig Wittgenstein: unpublished dictated typescript [a.k.a. *The Pink Book*], Papers of Ludwig Wittgenstein, Addition to the Von Wright Catalogue as GBR/0016/Add.Ms.407/I, Wren Library, Trinity College, Cambridge.

ACKNOWLEDGEMENTS

Thanks above all to Marjorie Perloff, who kept faith in this project. Joshua Beckman, Mónica de la Torre, Patrick Durgin, Miles Dworkin, Mike Golston, David Hobbs, Anne Jamison, Tim Knowles, Tom Mandel, Nick Nace, and Karla Nielsen were all generous and kind and encouraging — thank you. I hope your paths are all pinicolous, cool, and shaded.

KENNING EDITIONS

Juana I, by Ana Arzoumanian, translated by Gabriel Amor

Waveform, by Amber DiPietra and Denise Leto

Style, by Dolores Dorantes, translated by Jen Hofer

PQRS, by Patrick Durgin

Propagation, by Laura Elrick

Tarnac, a preparatory act, by Jean-Marie Gleize, translated by Joshua Clover with Abigail Lang and Bonnie Roy

Stage Fright: Selected Plays from San Francisco Poets Theater, by Kevin Killian

The Kenning Anthology of Poets Theater: 1945-1985, edited by Kevin Killian and David Brazil

The Grand Complication, by Devin King

Insomnia and the Aunt, by Tan Lin

The Compleat Purge, by Trisha Low

Ambient Parking Lot, by Pamela Lu

Some Math, by Bill Luoma

Partisan of Things, by Francis Ponge, translated by Joshua Corey and Jean-Luc Garneau

The Dirty Text, by Soleida Ríos, translated by Barbara Jamison and Olivia Lott

The Pink, by Kyle Schlesinger

Who Opens, by Jesse Seldess

Left Having, by Jesse Seldess

Grenade in Mouth: Some Poems of Miyó Vestrini, edited by Faride Mereb and translated by Anne Boyer and Cassandra Gillig

Hannah Weiner's Open House, by Hannah Weiner, edited by Patrick Durgin

Kenningeditions.com

TREE DRAWING - Scots pine on Easel, Buttermere shore #1 is a work by British artist Tim Knowles. It is one of a series of drawings produced using drawing implements attached to tree branches, the wind's effects on the tree's branches recorded on paper. Like signatures each drawing is unique and varies, depending on the characteristics and structure of the tree species, the individual tree and the weather conditions at that moment. Some of the Tree Drawings utilise a single branch, whilst others employ as many as 100 branches each with a pen attached to produce a large drawing.

The Tree Drawings are just one part of a wider practice, which utilizes chance in the production of the work. Knowles instigates actions the results of which are often unknown and uncertain. This engagement with chance is crucial to Tim Knowles' work, which is generated by apparatus, mechanisms, systems and processes beyond the artist's direct control. Akin to scientific experimentation, a situation is engineered in which the outcome is unpredictable, directed by the external forces. These operations or performances seek to reveal the invisible forces in the world around us and investigate the nature of hidden systems.

For more info please visit: www.timknowles.com

CRAIG DWORKIN is the author of over a half-dozen books of poetry, including, most recently: *Chapter XXIV* (Red Butte Press, 2013); *Alkali* (Counterpath, 2105); *12 Erroneous Displacements and a Fact* (Information As Material, 2016), and *DEF* (Information As Material, 2017). Despite their aesthetic diversity, these works all attempt to probe the limits of language by working from the *linguistic* — the impersonal, asemantic, chance motivations of material signifiers in structural relations — toward the *literary*: language in lush and enthused rhetorical flush. In addition to working as a literary critic and art historian, Dworkin teaches at the University of Utah and serves as Founding Senior Editor to the Eclipse Archive <eclipsearchive.org>.